Parenting Adult Children

How to Communicate Better with Your Grown Son or Daughter

By

Ann R. Sutton

Table of Contents

Introduction

Parenting adult children can be three times easier than you thought it to be. It all depends on your approach.

What are the challenges you face in parenting your adult child? How easy has the journey been?

Well, whether rocky as a mountain, or as plain as milk, you will always need the following ideas to have a better relationship with your grown-up child. Let me take you through.

When your child turns twenty-something

So, let's say that your twenty-two years old just came back from college and is hoping to pass a few months with you. But what happens if he is 26 and just lost his job, and came back to your place hoping to stay there until he puts himself together again? Dealing with this kind of situation can be very challenging for parents. Whether the child is 21 and never wanted to go to school for months or older and still staying at home, there is a lot of adjustments you have to do as a parent to get along. Most times, we ask ourselves as parents, how are we to manage the financial aspect? How will you manage the train before asking them to contribute? Also, what about cleaning the house? What if they do not want to abide by the rules? How long should we stay patient?

What truly happens to a child when he turns twenty-something?

Three months into the pregnancy, 90 per cent of mothers know what to expect. You know your legs will be swollen and very soon, you will have frequent fatigue. During the first few years of parenting, you know your child has to feed correctly and wear clean clothes. Well, the story is a lot different when the child turns twenty.

Dating, drinking and other supposed grown-up stuff will happen to your child. So, what exactly should you expect?

- **He will be 'enlightened.'**

Sitting, eating, talking and walking were the early education you gave to your child. Now, he has grown past that. Remember that as he grew, there were times he could not differentiate between number of times you made it a goal to get the right thing into his head. Now, things have changed.

Your once little boy can now get a date by just swiping his phone and order a pizza to his classroom without his phone. When he is drunk, he can find his way home with an

Uber even when he does not have a dollar or cent in his pocket.

That's a reduction in the list of things to make you worried. Technology has made common sense commoner.

- **Independence will be his next desire**

Yes, your grown child will want to move out of your house; he wants his own space. So, you should be prepared to let your little boy go. It is funny how hard this gets after wishing for your own space and private time with your spouse.

However, giving the grown kid his own space does not mean he will completely stay out of yours. One way or the other, he will find a way to arrive unannounced, if he cannot, your warm romantic night be interrupted with someone behind your Spotify.

Do not also be surprised when you come home to meet a party in your house when they do not even blink at seeing you at their door unannounced during a supposed emergency. It is easy to feel "oh God! I thought he moved out" but yea, you have to get used to it.

- **You will not just throw him off your payroll**

It is a difficult thing to cut your twenty-something off your payroll at once. They will continue to leach unto yours until they take you to a nursing home. Pray they do not borrow your car because they will never bring it back with gas. Once the vehicle is in their hands, be ready to fund their speeding ticket.

Never will you use your subscription alone. From Netflix to Amazon, to Spotify, they will sneak themselves in. It is funny how these happen.

- **The healthcare will still be your responsibility**

The child is off the waiting room for the paediatrician, but that does not mean that you will not have to find them a new doctor and medical insurance. The awaiting heartbreak from their medical call on an ignored stomach virus or flu will get you on your toe. Here, you will deploy your passion for nursing you left behind twenty years ago and suggest an over the counter treatment for them.

- **Record keeping**

They never seem to find anything. The same panic calls you got from school when they could not find their pen or book is still what you will be getting now. The only difference is that the current missing items will be much more expensive. Though this may not be for every kid, keep the emergency numbers of locksmiths handy as they will frequently misplace their keys; if not, phone or passport.

In case they forget their wallet in a place they cannot remember, do not overwork yourself, phone the bank and practice Lamaze breathing. Just like it worked for labour, it will help now that you are dealing with your kid in his terrible twenty.

Parenting strategies to adopt for kids at twenty-something

I know what it feels like to parent grown kids. At this stage of parenting, now that they are grown is more challenging seeing that they will have their ways of doing things which may not even relate to yours. When facing a challenge like this, try the following

- **Give them time to figure themselves out**

Young people, especially men, usually take a longer time to decide what they want from life. This decision is much easier for women. If you notice, most young guys do not stick with the first job they get out of college for many years. They tend to switch between jobs until they find a suitable one or one they think is perfect. If you find this in your son, get ready to have him knocking at your door now and then. This knock will not just be to come, visit and go back. It will be to spend time there for a little while; maybe a month or more.

To survive with this kind of child in your house, you have to understand that he needs time. So you are going to cut him some slack. Allow him the private time to think and do not be tempted to compare him if he does not land a job anytime soon.

- **Try not to lower your expectations of him or her**

No matter what happens, never lower your expectations of your children. Staying at your house is already a tough decision, and may make them anxious, depressed, or suffer from low self-esteem. However, this is not an affirmation for you to let go of your trust in his abilities. At this time, he needs you to be diligent and giving him hope, be loving, compassionate, and patient but also firm in your dealings with him.

With your hopes still high for him, he knows that there is an awaiting standard for him to measure up. Tell him that you understand the way things are with him, but that does not mean you will continue to manage him in his sub-standard state.

- **Encourage them. We do not know how hard they find it to stay at home with you**

Most young men have high expectations from their jobs, and this may cause them not to settle for just any job until they get one that meets their taste. When the child is going through this phase, encourage him with all the support you can. What he desperately needs is a shoulder to lean on while paying the price for his career. It is common for parents to lose patience and feel like their child is taking too much time to meet their goals and dreams. Even when you think this way, try not to let it show.

- **Try making them pay**

It may sound like love and very sensible to let children live in the house without contributing to anything. But letting them do that will only make them less responsible. A real man who wants to take care of stuff in the future will start small, even when in your house. So when next you want to pay the rent, try asking for some. It does not matter if it is that small. He can also throw in some money for the food every once in a while. Let him know when you are going to the grocery store and ask if he has anything to add.

If you are financially okay and do not need his money, save it up in the bank for him without his knowledge. As time goes on, or when he moves out of your house, you can then return it to him. You can also send it as a modest donation from you to him when he is in dire need of money.

- **Just three rules**

Getting a grown-up to abide by all your rules can be challenging and very frustrating. So, instead of trying to get him to obey all the rules, give him just three most important ones. If you are like me, you make those three a summary of everything he has to obey. These three rules should be focused on helping him become a better man.

The number one issue to take care of is his behavior. Let him know that he has to clean the house and help you out with some chores immediately he wakes up. The second can be his time of returning. This has been the reason many parents fight with their children. Let him know he cannot stay out of the house past midnight, and he does not have to speak to you rudely. If he must stay out late, a polite phone call will do. Let the third be whatever you choose. If you think your child does not want to abide by these rules, you can get him to sign the contract. If he does not, please show him the way out of your house.

- **Set a time frame**

It is not rude, but you cannot get your child living in your house forever. Right when he comes in and tells his reason for being back, let him know the duration he is allowed. If you are only comfortable for 3 to 6 months, let him know. This will inspire him to put himself together and get a job before then. When the duration is almost expiring, be a kind mother to give him a month or two reminders.

We aim to raise men, not grown-up kids who shy away from responsibilities. It sounds kind and loving to be over-generous with your kids, but do you know how much of the kids you spoil when you do this? It may be comfortable for us as parents, but we should know that it breaks the young men and make them weak. It also deprives them of their sense of responsibility, capability, and power. So, while rejoicing over the privilege for you to see and hold your child again, remember to be careful not to spoil him in the process.

What to tell your grown children when they become adults

It's like we never get to say enough when raising our children. And sometimes, we find this problematic as we are afraid of making them feel we are treating them like kids. So, instead of getting them to cringe on the sofa, walk into their room and casually give them this advice

1. **Make it a weekly duty to pay your credit card debt**

I hope you get a convenient day or time of the week to pay off your balance. If you do, teach your child to do the same. Credit card balance is never small, so it's better to pay it even if you own one cent. It will help you budget your spending, and prevent you from being charged a late payment fee. We all know that this is the surest way of staying out of credit card problems.

2. **Dress up**

It's better to be overdressed than underdressed. So, teach your children to know how to dress for the exact location. It does not have to be tuxedos; he just has to know how to wear matching outfits with the occasion. Do they know? Remind them again with this advice.

3. Wear a smile and be kind

Life may never be entirely kind for anyone. However, we cannot give our experience and chances of smiling and being kind to life. Let your child understand this and never feel like he's the only one going through troubles. There should be no criteria attached to being kind to anyone.

4. Always be mindful

Every situation is a result of little decisions and actions. So, one needs to be mindful about every step. Try not to get carried away with the moment, as it may cause you to miss out on outstanding opportunities without knowing it. Teach your children not to rush into important decisions.

5. Never give out all

Spending and giving out everything only leads to emptiness. At least, there should be something reserved for you. From money to privacy, and even love, there is always a need to withhold a little.

Saving money is an excellent way of paying yourself for a job well done. And every time you spend, you give away what you have, and he may end up having nothing left. So, first put it away. When you get used to doing this from now on, you'll be surprised how much it adds up within a short duration.

6. Start by starting

The principal failures in life are those that plan but never get to execute them. If you want to wait for the right time to do a thing, you will never do it. So if you're going to start, start. The most authentic way to start is by starting.

Also, the primary way to mastery is to continue at it. The more you speak, the more you will speak. The more you practice your new habits, the more they become a part of you. Do not forget that this also applies to bad habits. So, the next time you want to do it "just this once" remember, that it will intensify the difficulty for you to stop.

7. Be sure you love it

Most young men do not settle for what they do not like, and I apply that to myself. I particularly tell grown-ups this. Change your job if you think it is tedious or tiring. Leave an apartment if you do not feel comfortable. Refuse to waste your precious time enduring the situations you can change.

Pass it onto your child on my behalf. They can thank me later.

8. Keep them clean

Let them know that they will accomplish more in a day if they stay in a neat apartment. So when they wake up, let them ensure that their bed is dressed and your pillowcases are washed. Sweeping the floor will not kill them so they may want to try. About their underwear, allow them to do justice to them when they are tired of wearing them smelly.

9. Take responsibility

You know the saying he that fight and run away shall come back to fight another day. Well, whoever wrote this wasn't drunk on that day. It applies to every aspect of life. Advice, your child, to face his fears. Even when he screws up, encourage him to start anew. The earlier he faces his fears, the quicker he will master them.

10. Love

It costs nothing to love, but love is a commodity you owe everyone. It should start with his family. Yes, he may have some real friends who hold his hands when he is down and helps him get past the troubles; however, what they give to him cannot be compared to the unconditional love from a family.

I remember advising a young man who had ongoing issues with his parents and siblings. I told him "As long as you live on this earth, ensure you do all you can from your heart for your family. Else, will spend the rest of your life regretting it." More than I thought, his situation experienced a turnaround. Mama became happy, and so did everybody.

11. Let the email of the recipient be the last thing you fill out before sending an email

Many people had to pay dearly before learning this one. I cannot tell you the number of incomplete emails has been sent to people. Some even send emails to the wrong recipient.

Tell your child only to fill out the email of his recipient when the next thing on his mind is to click the "send" button. Else, he may end up sending a love letter to his boss.

12. Know that your parents love you beyond measure

Whatever you say here may be an understatement to your child until he has children of his own to love. Though they can be annoying sometimes, through the thick and thin, he will know that they make the world completely different.

When it comes to being parents, your love for your children is immeasurable. Let him know that this too is an understatement compared to how you feel about him.

Releasing your adult child

It is natural and healthy to bond with your child. However, there will come a time you will have to let them go, though not totally. This is usually a not so easy thing to do as many moms get too attached to their children until it becomes unhealthy.

It is possible and necessary to detach from and release your children when the time comes. Here, you will have to re-examine your dependencies and expectations and learn to see them making choices (even crazy ones) without letting it get so much to us. It is difficult to detach from your children, but with the right help, you will find a way to separate healthily.

Before learning how to separate and release our adult children, let us look at some of the reasons many mothers become too attached to their children:

- The need to be loved and needed
- The desire to nurture a person
- The desire to see our children love us back as a result of the love you have showered on them

These reasons, though vital to you as a mother, can short-circuit the flow of love between you and your adult child. This is because the adult child earnestly seeks for freedom and an opportunity to nurture himself. So, during your quest to hold your child close and watch him become the man you have always dreamt of, learn to let go.

How to release your grown-up child

A few months after you had your child, and even as you watched him grow and turn into an adult, all your concern has been to provide for him and support his character. However, it feels like a twinkle of an eye, and now you have to let him go. Now, you won't be concerned about his provision, and any of those areas that first got all your attention.

As a parent who had this responsibility dedicated to you, it is hard to switch focus from your cute little now-grown kids to allow them to run their lives. However, you can feel better about letting your grown child go with this.

Learn to trust

The problem is not with letting go of the child; it is trusting that they will be responsible enough to love and care for themselves when you are not around. So, if you learn to give them the benefit of the doubt, you could know whether you are right or wrong.

Whether you are right or wrong, the child will always have to learn by himself. So, letting the child act is a part of growth.

Whether or not you see a reason to trust your child, from his prominent ability to handle issues and take care of himself, you should comfort yourself with the fact that they have been able to manage to be fine since when they were kids.

Find a new way of bonding even when they are afar

Seeing a child in your house is not the only way you can bond with him. Learn to get used to talking on the phone, like when he was in college. However, try not to overdo it.

Allow the child some space, and he will naturally come to you when he gets into trouble or needs help dealing with problems adults face.

Hold onto them in prayer

Letting go of a child can be challenging. After they move out, you may spend the first week crying and feeling like you heard them call your name when they are not around. Sometimes, you may be tempted to prepare lunch awaiting their return only to realize that they won't. If they do, it is just to stop by and say hi.

Sure, instead of being so helpless and feeling like you do not have control over your child, hold onto him in the place of prayer. Pray for him and ask God to help guide and direct him. That is when you will have an assurance of peace and know that he is being led by the Almighty to take care of himself.

When you do, with the imagination that your grown child has turned a particular way, do not assume they will make the wrong decisions. Believe your prayer worked and watch it work.

When your adult child ignores you

It can be more than devastating to see the child you love and spent all your energy and resources to raise not give you a cent of love. It is not common for grown children who ignore their parents to feel guilty. This is the primary reason they continue in the act for so long.

The relationship between parent and adult children usually weaken their bonds and usually cause adverse effects on the family.

The first thing to do when you suspect your child is ignoring you is being certain of whether or not the child is genuinely ignoring you.

Sometimes, children spend lesser time with their parents because they have lesser time on their hands. Hectic schedules are one of those reasons parents may misunderstand the distance.

To know if your child is ignoring you, look out for the following signs:

Signs your child is ignoring you

1. They never call you by themselves

Parents are usually drowned in the love they have for their children, and this can push them to call several times a week. This can put you in a tight corner and not let you know if your child is putting to communicate with you.

Take some time out to examine your call log to see how many times you have called your child this week, and how many times the first called you to start a conversation.

If you are always the first person calling, then know that your child does feel it is important to talk to you; takes you for granted; or does not want to make any effort towards building a good relationship. Do not defend them; no one is too busy to love.

Also, investigate to be sure that every time your children call, it is not just to get help from you. Yes, we are used to the parasitic relationship as parents, but this is not meant to be the same forever.

A child that loves and respects you will call you regularly to be sure you are in good health. If you notice this, there is no doubt that your thoughts are right.

2. They do not visit you until you push

This is mostly applicable to people who have their children living within the same geographical region. If your child is living a 30-minute drive away from you and you do not get to see him regularly, suspect ignorance. An absence without getting you informed of any serious schedule he has in his hands; is a glaring sign that he is avoiding you or not just interested in being with you.

It is an entirely different case if the child is living very far away like a foreign country or something, but if this is the case, the child will still find a way of reaching out to you. This is not the 18th century when there were no phones.

Though the case is never the same for everyone, you know your child, and you will be able to feel when the child is living with his separate family feeling happy, and not wanting you in the picture.

3. You will only hear about the occurrences in their lives from outsiders

Except you pushed your children away, they will always want to share with you, and the milestones they accomplish in life. So, if you are not enlightened about the current occurrences in your child's life, it could be that they are ignoring you.

Learning that your child moved to a new city with his family, or just got a mega promotion from work, from an outsider is terrible. It is great news that shouldn't be kept away from the family. When these decisions are made without him consulting or telling you about it at its peak stage; it means that your child is ignoring you or has no respect for you.

If what you hear is bad news, it could be that they do not want to bother you, or if your health was quite unstable, that means they just want to save the information for the right time to share it.

4. They cook up excuses for missing important events

Oh! The puppy fainted, and he had to immediately rush him to the vet doctor only to find out he is pregnant. Wow! What an excuse! Stories similar to this is, or worse is what you will get when your child is trying to stay away from you. They just won't remember the birthday. If they do, then it's either their boss from work stopped them from coming or they only had a whole lot of babysitting to do.

I am not saying that your children can be so busy that they forget or miss an important event with the family. This is really possible it can be true but if it happens more than once twice or thrice, know that there is something wrong somewhere. Missing Easter and Christmas simultaneously is a sign that there is something fishy.

5. They act rebellious towards you

At first, they will think you are boring. Later, it will develop into hate.

Every grown child knows he has to respect and listen to his parents' advice. If your child disobeys or thinks you are just too old to make sense, know the child despises you, and this led him to ignore you.

For instance, if you suggest a right school where he can take your grandchildren too, and he bluntly refused without giving a

strong reason, know that there is a strand of
hatred in there.

Reasons your grown child may ignore you

Being ignored by a person you love is like giving a hard punch on a rock. You will never escape feeling the pains. This is the same thing that happens to your child when he loves you deeply. So, if this child that is biologically programmed to love you stays away from you or avoid your calls for weeks or even months, then it is caused by something very severe, severe enough to make them prefer feeling the pains of being away from you. Let's look at some of them:

1. You mistreated them during childhood

The best time to build bonds with a child is during his early childhood. If you did not have so much time to spend with him, or you make him feel less important, there is an excellent chance that he will ignore you when he is grown. This may not be his fault; when the bond is not there, it is difficult for him to force it.

Also, if you were abusive to your child during early childhood, it will build the resentment in them which they will grow with. It will be a little challenging if not impossible to change their minds now.

Early childhood is a great defining moment for every child. It shapes their personality, and, hence defining a significant part of your future. If you were not usually there for your child, he must have to find a way to live comfortably without you. It will take too much effort for the child to learn to share their lives with you now.

2. You do not respect their private lives

Getting in too deep into matters that do not concern you in their house can be a turnoff. To you it maybe just a common concern; however, it is far more different for your child and his partner.

It is okay to want to spend time with each other a little more, but it is terrible and very wrong to become clingy. They have their lives, and you have to understand that.

3. You still consider them as kids

You undermine your child's value every time you see him as just a kid. Parents become culprits of this scenario very quickly. Though you may not know, every time you take out his car without his permission, try to make decisions for him, or not value his work, you make him feel less like a man and will cause resentment to accumulate in his heart. As time goes on, he will want to go farther and farther from you.

4. You hate their spouses

Your child definitely values his spouse and will want you to do the same. If you do not like this spouse in person, you need to respect her for your child's sake.

Many families find it difficult to welcome new people and open their heart to them. However, marriage makes them officially your child's partner and significant other. So, you have to find a way to deal with what you feel inside.

When your child notices that you do not have this liking for his spouse, he will try to avoid a clash between you two, and this will lead to the unnecessary distance.

So, when next you are tempted to despise your child spouse, remember that it can cost you his love.

5. You always want to have the final say

Let me say you are controlling. Or maybe you are not, but always wanting your decision to be the final, is a no-no. No one wants to feel stupid around his mum. So, even if you do not feel so comfortable with other people's options, learn to try them out.

Acting bossy can be another reason. This can be an easy loophole seeing that you were once the boss in the house, running the show. Now, your kids are all grown and the least thing he wants to see is you acting that way in front of them and their kids.

What if your grown-up child makes a wrong decision?

It is easier to prevent a younger child from making a mistake than an adult. Some adult children do not even consider their parents' advice as useful, because they see them as old, and not updated with the trend. But as parents, we get to wonder and feel bad when our children do not listen to our opinions not to talk of applying them.

When your child goes ahead to do what you warned them against, they invite into their lives adult-sized problems like addiction to drugs, and sex, and even disappointments too great for them to handle. Some may even land in prison, God forbid!

Children not taking your opinion does not mean you presented them the wrong way. In fact, most of the time when your adult child does not apply your advice; it has nothing to do with you. Though it's excruciating to see your adult child with "no you" in your opinion, there are still some things you can do. Though prevention may not be possible, it is never too late to redeem the situation.

How to handle your child's poor decision

The challenge in parenting an adult-child doubles when the child does not listen and keeps making poor decisions. This calls for extra work; there is a higher chance of succeeding if you and the child have better communication and understanding.

- **Stay out of the situation**

Since he's your child, he may feel entitled that you remedy the situation at hand. Doing this is good, although you are not helping the child. Your aim is to raise a full-grown man that can stand up for himself at anytime and anywhere.

You love your child and you hate to see him suffer, but you should build up straight boundaries and set consequences when a person breaks it.

For you, setting this boundary and consequences may be letting your child not have access to the house when be hasn't sought help for his addiction, or not giving him more money to pay off his excess credit card debt.

This is a somewhat helpful way to love your child. You do this once; they will know better than turning a deaf ear.

- **Do not be that one-stop help this time**

Reducing the effects of the consequences of your children's mistakes remind them to feel less of the heat their situation caused. And they may get back to it again after the one time.

Mistakes come with crises so allow them to experience theirs. At least if they do not learn from your advice, they will remember them from the price they pay for the mistake. Try not to feel the pain of their crisis like they do. Pretend like you are not moved by it and let them experience the consequences alone.

You cannot continually pay for someone else's wrongs.

• Keep holding onto your standards

You should not adjust your standard to suit an irresponsible child. Even when you feel like you are going to die from the heartbreak, hold on to your standards and do not let go of them to meet your child where he is. Else, you will keep adjusting your standard until you have no standards left. To have a balanced parent-child relationship, let your child grow up to meet you where you are. She will need to thank you for his life and family.

However, by doing this, you will get to know your child beyond what is causing you pain. A piece of in-depth knowledge and a better relationship with the child can get him to change his mind and make a turnaround.

• Model your expectations

Just like when they were kids, your children do what you do most of the time. You cannot tell your adult child not to smoke when you have a cigarette in your hand. That would be you being a hypocrite. You want them to be financially responsible? Show them that it is possible.

But this is the most powerful tool; most parents tend to overlook it. So, when next you want your child to bring home a golden trophy, show them what it means to be diligent and hard-working.

- **Manage the frustration**

The natural thing everyone does when they are frustrated is to lash out with very grievous words. This, however, is usually not the best thing. If you feel you need to talk about the situation, and sure you are not just pouring out the way you think on them. It will only cause them to resent you the more thereby keeping more distance.

No matter how bad the situation gets, still be his number one cheerleader. Building a relationship and strong trust with the children is more important than venting your anger. If you still want to pour out the wrath, go to a trusted friend and not your child.

- **Avoid over-thinking about the situation**

Right from when they were babies, we always had this feeling and need to bear the pain so that they can be free. However, it is not even possible to do that. So, you just cannot kill yourself over what you cannot change. It is best for you to get back to your good friend and better relationships right now.

Become a member of a support group to help you out. You can go to your church, or support groups with parents also dealing with irresponsible children. They will help you put yourself together, and find a solution to your son's problems. If you have any problem yourself, they will also help you fix it. A shoulder to lean on can a be all you need so go get it.

- **Pray about it**

I do not know what you believe in, but for me, this is usually the first line of action. If you are to name only one person in this world that loves our children more than we do, it is God. So, when your child is falling into the path of thorns, release him to God's hands for God to pull him out.

No matter what you go through with your child, love is the ultimate. It is like a soothing balm for every illness. So, no matter your method of disciplining your child for falling out of the way, ensure you do it from the standpoint of love and understanding.

How to manage disrespect from your adult child

It is not very easy to deal with a child that does not give you the respect you deserve as a parent. Having a toxic child is less-than-expected, and is usually a very frustrating behavior to handle.

Though every grown child has his responsibilities, stresses, and disappointments, it is required of them to handle their stress the right way. So, do not be blinded into believing that you should swallow any disrespect from your child because he is having a rough time.

The offence is straightforward to reach when your child does not respond the way you expected after all the stress of raising them. However, dealing with them with the offence mindset will keep you and him far from achieving the kind of relationship you want. Coping with a disrespectful grown child has so much to do with first understanding where the disrespect is coming from

When your child treats you less than you expect, handle the situation with the following tips.

1. Have a deal

Having a deal is a great way to earn constant respect from your child. Set clear boundaries, and let him know that you will not blink whenever he insults you. Though you are going to have a good healthy relationship with him, let him know how far he can go and the aspect of your life he cannot tamper.

If after the boundaries, he still gets back to being disrespectful, stick to your word and do what you promised. In this aspect, it's no different from raising a teenager. When he knows what the consequences will be, he should not be surprised when you deliver them.

2.   Try to be less reactive

Oh! Kids love it when they know they can get you barking when they want. They know they have control over you and your mind and will not stop at anything until they annoy the life out of you. Being reactive will bring you down to their level and give them permission to disrespect you the more. This is no different from what teenagers and toddlers do.

When the disrespect comes, the first thing you should do is to take a deep breath. That will settle you and give an idea of how well to handle the situation. Children get paralyzed when you handle a problem the way they least expected. Be silent when he really wants you to bark, and quit tolerating when he thinks you are just going to keep quiet and look at him.

Try not to speak in the heat of the anger. It could ruin everything and leave negative indelible marks in their lives. You would not want that to happen.

3.   Acknowledge their emotion

Letting them know you understand how they feel will make them realize how they truly feel. This will bring distress to hold if the child is responsible. When you tell your child 'i know you are outraged,' or 'it must be tough for you to deal with this,' you go a step ahead of calming down their anger, and making them more likely to reason the right way. Most times, all you need to diffuse the argument is just a simple validation.

4.   Try seeing from his point of view

The most typical cause of misunderstanding is the difference in perspective. We could all be saying the same thing in different words and fighting against each other for not understanding. Maybe your child is right, and maybe you are. Take a second look at the situation and put yourself in the shoe of a twenty-five-year-old who is either frustrated or just trying to find his way around life.

5.   Investigate the hostility

People do not just wake up one blessed morning and decide to be hostile. There is something inside that brings about the hostility and will grow to a point where it can be made manifest. To see why your child is reacting the way he is, find out what is going on deep down him.

The problem could be you, no parent is perfect, though some make a more severe mistake than the others.

Also, the child's hostility can come from a frustration with their broken relationship or work. Sometimes, they are pushed to lash out on the parents. I hope you understand the point because I am not asking you in any way to tolerate their inconsistencies. After all, they are hurt. I'm saying that it could be easier for you to manage the situation when you know why your child just suddenly changed into being hostile and disrespectful.

6.   Talk about it

Sometimes, putting yourself in their shoes will get you to really see what they are going through. Here, you will understand the basic of talking to your child effectively. Our understanding is that you've got to deal with this disrespectful behavior. Ask your child where it's coming from and why he just cannot stop doing it. Here, you may get to hear the things you never knew were bothering them as some children can have a high level of secrecy.

The manner of approach to use here is significant. Understand that if you go to your child like you are seeking for a fight, you will get a fight but if you go as a friend that is willing to reconcile, he will be more willing to confide in you.

Also, know that there may be situations where your child backs out no matter how friendly you appear. They may not want to get involved in the discussion or out-rightly insult you again. In this case, you have to go back and enforce the rules. If it must be a power tussle, then gird your loins and be ready to fight.

Fighting here does not mean being at a keen edge to give it to your child when he really wanted. Sometimes it could just be a silence when he wants to hear you scream. However, still, be kind to your child though you are not nice. You do not have to look nice. Mother, do what you should to put a smile on your face.

7.   **Treat him like a buddy**

Most parents make the mistake of treating our 30-year-old children like they are kids. You are not wrong if you do this. They are your kids but this time, the grown-up kind. Every grown-up child will appreciate it when you treat him as a friend.

 So, when he disrespects you do what you would do to your friend. Say how you feel to them, and cut contact if you must.

With the contacts off, it should not take forever to get back together. If he apologizes, forgive him and continue from where you stopped. If he does not, still forgive him after a few weeks. Know that you are not set out to punish him; all you are trying to do is to get him to treat you the right way.

When you get to talking with him again, try to build a deeper relationship this time. When your relationship deepens, the unspoken truth will be revealed, and there will be a better understanding between you two.

There are usually times when your child will work out their lives and see how they can meet up with your colleagues. This may cause them to misbehave. However, you should know when your child is trying to blame you for his misery when you are genuinely not responsible.

Also, you know a whole lot of young people have too much pressure for them to handle. Their friends brag about their achievement and touch and intimidation occurs, especially if he is trying to get something to do. It is harder to get an excellent job with an unstable mind; social media is not even helping matters. So, amid the pain and disrespect you feel on the inside, understand that not everyone knows how to manage pressure and disappointment.

8.   Know when it is a mental illness

Most parents do not understand when their children have a mental illness until it becomes severe. In the present era, there is a rise in mental ailments among young people. And people with mental illnesses do not have good ways of communicating it with their loved ones. So, if your child is psycho, they may put you in a place where they treat you less than you deserve.

Before backing out to tick right for yourself on the discipline checklist, try to put yourself in your child shoes and understand their pain for a moment. Is there anything you are there dealing with that you do not see? If you find any, help your child get through it. But if you do not, talk to your child, you never can tell what's bothering him.

9.   Set some rules

Boundaries are essential to protect you from a toxic child. Sorry, I had to use the word 'toxic' but then, what do you expect me to call the child that won't stop disrespecting you?

Set the rule that he is likely to respect. If it means setting rules that will throw him out of the house the next time he disrespects you, please do it. It is essential for your health, both physically and psychologically.

10.   Take a break

There are situations where nothing you do will be tagged right in the eye of your child. This means that it cannot work out no matter how much you try. This is very common with children who do not have compatibility living styles or personalities with their parents. If this case is yours, then know that it is almost impossible to stay under one roof with such a child for a long time.

Show commitment to have a better relationship with this kind of child. You must stay away from each other at least within some months. Even research proves that there is no harm in taking a break from one relationship. A reasonable break can strengthen the relationship more than staying together.

11.   Get a counsellor

Parents face very many problems with their adult children. So, the few we've written here is not enough to tell you what to do or how to handle your specific situation. At certain level, getting a counselor can be of great help.

Consult as many counsellors as you can. If you realize that your child has a mental problem, advise him to visit a psychiatrist or psychologist. Getting through this road can be very difficult. So, you must help yourself out by joining a parent support group instead of keeping the issue to yourself.

Bonding with your disrespectful adult kid

A child is always cherished no matter what they do. It is not too late to bond with your child after being through a turbulent season. The steps below have been found to help children feel at ease with their parents. When the ease is in place, the quality of the relationship between them will improve.

Though they do not work like magic, applying them diligently and allowing time can help you win back the child you thought you lost to disrespect.

1. Replace the lost value

The primary reason children rebel is when they believe they do not have value in the house. So, to restore the situation, replace the lost value. Make them feel like they are highly esteemed and needed in the family.

Achieving this is pretty easy. Start by asking their opinion and thoughts before taking some little actions. Do not just seek the opinion, accept them and apply, and they will have a sense of worthiness and value in the home and your life too.

Appreciate them for what they do, value their private life, family and work. Learn how to give them the kind of respect you think should be given to you.

Also, address them with the utmost respect when their children are present. And try not to hurt their esteem when you are angry.

2. **Value their time**

Understand that your children have other things to do, to have your kids total love and care, you have to understand that they are trying so hard to divide their time. With the wife and children in his life, it will be hard for him to give all his time to you.

Ask if they are free to help you with a request. They have a professional life, and it may not be so easy for them to let go of a full day. With this, I am not saying that you should stay away entirely for asking for their help. Enjoy the time they give you and show them you really do. This will make them create even more time for you in the future.

3. **Tell them how you feel**

I am yet to know of any other method that will replace this in solving problems, especially in the family. This discussion is usually better when done one-on-one, as every aspect of the communication will be involved. The child will get to see your facial expressions and gestures; he will understand that it is coming from your heart.

The talk does not have to be a strategic or a written down speech. You can just ask them how they are and how they feel about the gap between you two. At first, the child may not want to talk about it so much. But if you take the lead and tell them how you feel genuinely without being judgemental, they will be free to open up to you.

Being vulnerable before them will push them to express the hidden love and care in their heart for you automatically bringing them emotionally close. Be vulnerable, not manipulative.

4. Listen to them

This is not a very serious conversation like an interview, so you have to take it lightly and also allow them to talk too. This will make the conversation much more meaningful. Let it not just end with the discussion, spend time with each other.

Take a walk or go fishing with your son and discuss other things like his family, plans, and games. Ensure the discussion is detailed and fun. As they listen to you, listen to them genuinely and attentively. This will free up the jam-packed negative energy between you two.

5. Right your wrong

Maybe your child disrespected you because you do not like their spouse and children, or perhaps you are just too hard towards them. Getting them back will require you to like the children and his partner as well.

Allow him some privacy with his wife and children and not insist on following them everywhere they go. I know that it would have been fun to go for every picnic with your son, say no to some and allow him to have some private time with his family. Every child appreciates a mother that will enable him to have a little bit of fun.

6. Support them

It is very soothing to know someone has your back for real; even your children feel this way. Without your knowledge, your kid even grown-up looks up to you as an assistant and advisors. To them, your help is indispensable and they will follow it to handle some issues. This will make them feel like you genuinely care about them and what they do, and they will come back seeking you the more.

It will make a child start feeling guilty about staying away from you all this while and later, it will be the cord that binds your love forever.

When your child is getting married

So much joy accompanies the news of the engagement of either your son or daughter. But behind this joy is a secret fear of how the partner is and how long do marriages last. You are not alone in this fear seeing that statistics show that one out of two American marriages ends in divorce. However, it is still possible to be hopeful since there is a chance to have one that lasts forever.

There are chances are you are not the only person having this fear. Your child probably has them too. So it is time for you to wear a smile, and help a child get through the process with hope.

Maybe you had the not-so-good experience with your child's potential partner before the wedding day; this is not a time to remember. This person is about to be with your child forever, and you need to create a room in your heart for them.

Encouraging your child to the wedding process can prepare the child psychologically for a happy marriage. Among the things you have to do, the following advice is suitable for their wedding day.

Advice to prepare your children for their marriage

I know I think this advice is to prepare children for their wedding, but I'd like to see them as the advice you give to your child while he or she is getting dressed. If you have limited time for this, take a night before the wedding to have the discussion.

1. **Offer hope**

Regardless of how long your marriage lasted, encourage your child and make them see, one can have a long-lasting happy marriage. Taking responsibility for your mistakes and wishing you had corrected them earlier can be an excellent way to encourage your child to sit up and make his or her marriage work.

Show your child that even in a world where marriage is seen to be unimportant, that utmost joy can be derived from his union. Even when yours didn't work out well, let your child know that it is possible to be married to a human being, not just a jerk.

2. **Be focused on loving**

Problems in marriage usually start when one partner is focused on dragging the other into the right way or supposedly right way. This problem, however, is easily solved or prevented by just being focused on loving your partner. Like my mum would say, the best way to change a person is to love them the way they are. When they see that they received true love from you, they will be encouraged to adjust and make you feel better and happier to be with them.

Teach your child not to switch on the picture mode when something goes wrong in the marriage. That is good to discuss and talk about things; every discussion should create a platform of love and not condemnation or judgement.

3. **It does not have to be hike free**

It does not have to be totally made of honey before it is sweet. Even some sugar-coated foods are enjoyed. What I'm saying is that your child should not expect a trouble-free marriage no one ever gets one. Instead, let him or her make up his mind to stay with the partner through thick and thin. That is what true love does.

You can also share with a child the possible landmines to look out for in marriage. You may want to teach them about the excellent and bad decades. They deserve to be prepared.

4. **Compromise**

Sooner or later, the fairy-tale love will fade. So teach your children to be prepared to face marriage and all its unflattering realities. There will be times when they have to ask their partner this profound questions and should be ready to answer some themselves. However, this will start with you.

Right from their late teenage years to early adulthood, the mode of conversation will change. It will be more of a give and take, so be ready to show them how. It will need a little bit of vulnerability and trust. If you had a divorce, your child may ask you how and why it happened. This is usually the right time to tell your child the truth. However, it does not mean you should tell the whole story. You can decide what is private to you and what you say out while you keep the lien open.

With your child standing at the altar with someone entirely strange to you about to make them their significant other, there is more for you to ponder about than what to say.

The most important thing is how you open up your mind to receive the new person coming to your family as this is important to your child as it is to their spouse.

They are great chances that the child's partner will be less than your expectation. Maybe he or she has more tattoos than you expected, or does not even have a job. You have to prepare your mind to give them the ultimate love that they deserve as a person.

Conclusion

Having adult children makes the later part of life more enjoyable. However, reaching out to achieve that part of the joy is usually difficult.

During the early years of parenting, it usually feels like you have a thousand and one tasks to do and your children contribute to 90% of them. Now, it is time to love yourself and sneak around with your spouse as you have always dreamt off.

Letting go is never easy, but having a great relationship with them after they are gone makes the whole difference. Make their early years wonderful so that your last days will be.

Other Books by The Same Author

- <u>How to Teach ADHD Kids: Simple Parenting Strategies to Train and Discipline the Brain of Hyperactive and Impulsive Children</u>

- <u>How to Deal with Toddlers Tantrums: Powerful Techniques to Handle Persistent and Severe Attitudes in Toddlers (A Blueprint for Kid Behavior Management)</u>

- <u>246 Conversation Starters for Family Discussions: Start Dinner Conversation with Your Child, Get Them to Listen More, Improve Social Intelligence & Responsibility</u>

- <u>Parenting A Toddler: How to Get a Child to Listen and Follow Directions</u>

- <u>How to Teach Your Kid Responsibility: Powerful Techniques for Getting Your Kid to Behave, Learn and Grow into A Self-Reliant Adult</u>

- <u>How to Teach Toddlers to Talk: Ultimate Strategies to Get Your Kid to Start Talking and Developing a Proper Social Skills</u>

www.ingramcontent.com/pod-product-compliance
Lightning Source LLC
Chambersburg PA
CBHW031219160726
47992CB00006B/2816